Ghost Physics
Compelling Evidence for a New Theory

J.C. Knight

DEDICATION

This book is dedicated to my sister Fran, whose special gift
opened my eyes to the possibility of better understanding
the cycle of life and death that eventually affects us all.

CONTENTS

PREFACE

If you are reading this, then you probably have at least some interest in the field of paranormal activity and events. I do not claim to be an expert in this field, and in fact I do not believe anyone actually is. There simply hasn't been enough real scientific research into this field to provide sufficient evidence. However, we do have an abundance of knowledge that has been gained over the years in the fields of science and medicine, and I believe the most recent discoveries may now shed some light on this interesting topic. As I said, I am not a paranormal expert. My background is in science. I hold a doctorate in medicine. I am a licensed physician, although I have retired from practicing medicine and now teach chemistry, physics, advanced anatomy & physiology and pathology at both Master and Doctorate levels.

I wrote this book for two reasons. First to apply facts of medicine and physics to offer an explanation from a scientific standpoint of what a ghost may actually be; and second to raise awareness that more real scientific research is needed in this field. Socrates, the classical Greek philosopher and one of the founders of Western Philosophy once said "The only true wisdom is in knowing you know nothing." That is a simple yet powerful statement. It means that we don't know everything; that there is always something more for us to learn or discover. It's the whole reason that organizations like NASA and CERN were built. So that we could research and experiment to learn more about our universe and everything in it, from the largest farthest celestial objects to the smallest subatomic particles known to man. Since their induction, we have gained volumes of knowledge through theory and experimentation, and now know more than ever before. But we still don't know everything, and so the work continues.

When radio waves were first discovered back in the 1880s, they weren't called "radio waves" because back then radios didn't exist. In fact, no experimental machinery or equipment to produce radio waves existed yet. It all started in the 1860s with just a theory, put forth by an English scientist named James Clerk Maxwell. After observing the behavior of electrical fields and magnetic fields, he noticed a relation between the two. He realized that changing a magnetic field could induce an electrical field to form and vice versa. He theorized that coupling these fields together could produce electromagnetic waves. Later, in 1886 a German physicist named Heinrich Hertz applied Maxwell's theory to the production and reception of electromagnetic (radio) waves using two rods to serve as a receiver and a spark gap as the receiving antennae. A spark would jump where the waves were picked up. Hertz showed in his experiments that these signals possessed all of the properties of electromagnetic waves, and further proved that the electromagnetic fields would detach from wires and travel freely through the air as Maxwell's waves.

This was the birth of wireless communication. Most electronic items you use today, such as your cell phone, tablet or laptop exist because of this discovery and others like it. Imagine if these men had never come up with that theory, or an experiment to test it. We would not have wireless anything! No cell phones, no internet, no Bluetooth or any other wireless communications or services. Our world has progressed very far from the technology of the 1800s because of theory and experimentation. But there is more yet for us to discover, and not just in the field of technology. With more scientific theory and experimentation into the field the paranormal, we could begin to discover things we have only imagined. In this book, I would like to offer a new theory which may begin to pave the way for a better understanding of paranormal physics.

New discoveries in the field of quantum physics are starting to shed some light on what has, until now, remained unexplained. There is a great deal of information available on the paranormal, but there needs to be more exploration of the real science behind ghosts, the real physics of it.

In the field of physics research, there are two types of physicists: Theorists and Experimentalists, like Maxwell and Hertz. The Theorists put forth new theories that attempt to explain everything we observe in nature. The Experimentalists are the ones who build the machines to test the theories. For example, in the 1960s Theorists hypothesized a particle never before seen called the Higgs boson. For more than forty years it was only a theory, with no proof, until Experimentalists built the machines at the European Organization for Nuclear Research, known as CERN, that actually detected it, and changed everything we know about particle physics. Amazing new discoveries in science, like the Higgs, come first from new theories.

I would consider myself a type of theorist in that I would like to propose a new theory on what a ghost is, based on known and new scientific findings in the fields of standard and quantum physics and medicine. The internet itself was invented at CERN in 1989 so physicists could share their newly discovered data worldwide. I believe all scientific discovery starts with theory, and I have decided to write a book to share some new theories in hopes that further experiments might eventually be conducted to someday reveal what we can now only hypothesize about regarding the as of yet unknown.

1 A NEW THEORY

What is a ghost? There are many theories but the
only one that really makes sense is the one that's
supported by scientific facts. Currently, there are
five conventional theories, which are covered later in
this book. After nearly a year and a half of
exhaustive research, I have come up with the newest,
and what I believe is the most accurate theory of all
based on three extremely important scientific and
medical findings. My theory is this: When a person
dies, part of their physical brain is converted to pure
energy and leaves the body as a conscious
singularity. In other words, a 'ghost' is a conscious
singularity composed of the disembodied
consciousness of a deceased person in the form of
new mass less energy. It is similar to, but as I will
explain, much more accurate than the existing

theories. The existing theory I'm referring to specifically is the one which states that ghosts are the spirits of people who have passed away. For thousands of years people have believed this, and it is likely true, but it lacks scientific explanation. What exactly is a spirit? Until now, no one has been able to answer this scientifically, but I believe I can.

A spirit is the same thing as a ghost, which is also the same thing as a disembodied conscious singularity. In other words, it is the consciousness of a deceased person in the form of massless energy that has left their body. There are three vital scientific facts that support this theory. Two are very recent findings in the field of quantum physics, and the third is a previously unlinked medical research result. It's when you connect the dots of these three facts that it all starts to make sense.

The first supporting fact is the recent discovery by CERN scientists of the Higgs boson particle, also sometimes referred to informally as 'the God particle'. It is the particle responsible for the transfer of matter to energy and vice versa. It is described as a scalar particle force carrier in physics. (In Einstein's equation $E=mc2$, matter and energy are interchangeable and can neither be created nor destroyed, only transferred). The Higgs is what gives particles their physical mass.

The second is the recent discovery of OOR
(Orchestrated Objective Reduction), which
measures, for the first time, quantum energy
vibrations embodied as helical patterns in the
microtubules of the human brain; representing
human consciousness. Even more interesting is the
fact that this quantum energy was found to have the
ability to leave the body by converting from the
microtubules to a pattern of pure mass less energy.
Upon this conversion to a pure energy state, a small
amount of mass is lost from the body. It is the Higgs
boson that transfers part of the microtubule mass
from the body back to the Higgs field at the time of
death. (the Higgs field is a field discovered in
quantum physics that is discussed later in this book).

The third supporting fact of my theory is a set of
formally documented medical research findings by a
group of five physicians which took place at the turn
of the century, a time when very little was known in
the field of quantum physics. The lead research
physician was a man named Dr. Duncan
MacDougall. Dr. MacDougall theorized that the
human soul might have an actual measurable weight.
He obtained consent from several terminally ill
patients who agreed to participate in the research.
For each patient, Dr. MacDougall's group measured
an instant loss of approximately 21 grams of weight
at the exact moment of death, which, until now could

not be explained.   At the time, they did not know of the existence of the Higgs boson; or its ability to transfer matter.   Nor did they have any knowledge of OOR (Orchestrated Objective Reduction).   However, we now know about both of these, and can clearly see the connection which explains the loss of 21 grams of mass at the time of a person's death, confirming that something does leave the body instantaneously when a person dies.   This gives us new insight into what a ghost is.

Once discorporated from the body, the conscious singularity exists in the form of pure unseen energy. Under the right conditions however, the Higgs boson particle can temporarily impart a small amount of mass back to the singularity, enabling limited physical properties which result in variable forms of manifestations that we witness as ghosts, or paranormal events.

2 VISIBLE MANIFESTATIONS

By far, the most gripping event people report is a
visible manifestation, of which there are several
types. There seems to be no rhyme or reason as to
when or where you might see a ghost. Although
some locations are reported to be haunted, there is no
guarantee that if you go there you will actually see or
experience anything. Why is this? The answer lies
with what we know about the conscious and
subconscious. As previously explained, our
conscious has recently been attributed to quantum
vibrations found in helical patterns in the
microtubules of our brain cells, which can leave the
physical body. The massless energy particles that
compose the conscious, subconscious and emotional
states have the ability to interact with other particles
such as the Higgs. Once discorporated from the

body through Higgs boson interaction, the conscious goes into a less aware state, much like being in a dream. In a dream we can see and hear things, but don't pay much attention to them. In a dream you sometimes see things that don't make any logical sense at all. For example, you dream of someone you know, but they look like someone else; or you are in one place in a dream at one moment, and suddenly in another location the next - but you don't seem to pay much attention to it while you're dreaming. You may even look different in your own dream. Often these things don't make any logical sense, but your mind just accepts it as reality and keeps going. Of course in reality if these things happened, your reaction would be much different. So, in a dream state, the conscious and subconscious seem to function a bit differently than they do in the real, physical world. When you're asleep, you don't realize you are dreaming. With a ghost, it is the same thing, except they are not dreaming, but dead, and do not realize it. The conscious singularity is in a dream state, and although conscious to some degree, may only be partially aware of the environment it is in, and therefore may or may not respond to objects and/or people in that same place. There is no sense of time either, so a ghost may exist in a place for a long time and not realize it at all. Think about normal dreaming. Do you ever sense a passage of time? Can you tell how long you've been asleep once you wake up (without looking at a clock of course). The answer for most of us is no. It is actually very difficult to know how long you've been asleep after you wake up, until something or someone indicates it to you.

Whether or not a ghost manifests and what it looks like depends on its level of conscious and subconscious thought as well as it's emotional states. There are several different types of manifestations in which the entity can be seen, make noises that can be heard, move actual physical objects (or touch people), manifest as an EVP recording, or even just a temperature change. It all depends on the three major factors: the conscious, subconscious (preconscious/unconscious) and emotional states. There are many different levels of consciousness and emotional states, and therefore various combinations are possible. When the right combinations occur, it causes a manifestation of some kind. What manifestation we experience depends on what levels of consciousness and emotion present in a conscious singularity at that moment when we are observing (or recording) it.

Before I explain which combinations cause such manifestations to occur, I would like to briefly explain consciousness itself, which in the most accepted western models of psychology is actually divided into three levels: the conscious, preconscious and unconscious (the latter two sometimes collectively being referred to as the subconscious).

The conscious mind includes everything that we are aware of at the moment. It involves rational thinking. The preconscious is the part of our mind that contains our memories. It is not always present in the conscious but can be accessed to retrieve memories at any time we need them. The unconscious mind includes thoughts, memories, urges, etc. repressed outside of our conscious awareness. Often times it consists of things one considers unpleasant or unacceptable. For example, feelings of anxiety, pain or conflict. Many believe the unconscious influences behavior, even though the conscious is unaware of it.

Emotions are the other factor and involve feelings, which are actually separate from conscious cognition. Conscious and subconscious cognitive thoughts are derived from the cortex while emotions come from the limbic system of the brain. Recall that these structures are composed of living neurons in the brain and that the microtubules in those neurons house the quantum helical vibrations that lose their mass upon death to become what we call a ghost, or conscious singularity. So when we die, we take with us our conscious, pre/subconscious and emotions.

When conditions are right, and certain conscious and emotional states are reached in specific combinations, we are then presented with a manifestation that can be witnessed as a ghost, or paranormal event. What are those conditions and combinations? It depends mainly on the conscious being alert and wakeful; with the subconscious more self-aware and the emotions in an increased state. If the conscious singularity of the deceased is in an aware or alert state, the subconscious tends to follow and be more aware of itself, having a somewhat organized self image. If these two conditions are met and the emotional state is increased, something will manifest as a recognizable apparition or event. On the other hand, if the conscious is less alert and more in a dream state, the subconscious will follow with a less self-aware and somewhat disorganized self image, resulting in an amorphic, abstract mist or shadow. If the emotional state is increased in either instance, one of these two things will manifest. If the emotional state is flat and melancholic, nothing will manifest despite the states of consciousness. This is why triggers are often an effective tool in provoking a manifestation or paranormal event.

Based on the levels of the conscious and emotional

states, one of three events can occur. Either nothing is manifest and nothing is witnessed, or something abstract like a mist or vapor is seen, or a recognizable apparition or paranormal event is observed. The subconscious self image is important because the more self aware it is, the more accurate the self projection is in detail. For example, ghosts that are seen clearly as full apparitions appear as the individual wearing clothing. One example of this was documented when a worker at the Hawthorn Retirement Home in England saw an elderly woman in a green striped dress come through a wall and float toward her before disappearing. She did not recognize her at the time, but later identified her in a photo album of residents. While the woman in the photo was wearing a different dress, Margaret Dawes, owner of the Home, remembered that this particular woman's favorite dress was indeed green striped, which the worker had reported seeing the apparition wearing.

Of course clothing doesn't have a conscious, but it is seen on the individual because of self imaging projection, likely their favorite clothing, or last thing they remember wearing. Sometimes it is a uniform depending on service or occupation and how, when or where they died. These full apparitions are the most interesting manifestations because they are the most detailed and recognizable of the deceased for us to see. Unfortunately, it is most common for the emotional state to be flat and melancholic, with no readily available manifestation. Why is this? Because when the conscious is discorporated from the physical body, it enters a dream like state. It is conscious and self aware to some degree, but will usually have a neutral level of emotion. It is the same as when you are asleep and dreaming. As stated earlier, in your dream you will see things that don't make any logical sense at all, but you ignore or accept them as normal and just continue moving on through your dream. Just as you don't know you're dreaming when you are; they don't know they're dead when they are. And it is difficult for them to realize this, because the mind cannot usually tell dreams from reality while in this state. This is why direct interactions with them is so rare. Try it yourself as an experiment to see if you can do it. The next time you lay down to sleep, try to realize you're dreaming once you've fallen asleep. It is exceedingly difficult to do, it's just how the mind works, in both a living state, and after death.

Although it is not impossible, it is very difficult to realize in the middle of a dream that you are in fact dreaming. Some people can and have experienced this, but only a very few. I myself have been fortunate enough to have experienced it, but only twice, out of many, many attempts. As stated before, that's just how the mind works. We do experience emotions in our dreams, but much of the time emotions take a backseat to cognition and we move through our dreams just accepting whatever crazy reality we see around us. It's usually a neutral, flat and level state of emotion. With a ghost, the same is true, and nothing manifests. However, sometimes emotional states can increase depending on what we are seeing or hearing at the moment. It is when the emotions are "stirred up" that a ghost manifests itself. The following flow chart is just a basic summary diagram of how it works:

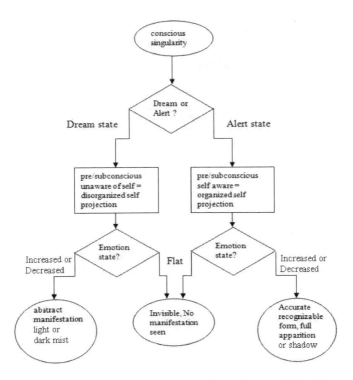

Of course ghosts don't follow a flowcharts, this all happens automatically, just like our autonomic nervous system which functions automatically in the living. Emotions invoke changes in the autonomic nervous system which results in automatic changes in the body. For example, when a living person is suddenly frightened by something, an immediate burst of epinephrine (adrenaline) is released from the medulla of the adrenal gland which has a profound effect on the physical body. The epinephrine binds to certain alpha and beta receptors in the body and extreme reactions occur. The heart rate rises and becomes stronger to circulate more blood to the body; the airways dilate to let more oxygen into the lungs; the pupils dilate to let more light into the eye. Some of the blood vessels in the body constrict to raise the blood pressure; while others such as those running through the skeletal muscle dilate to increase blood flow and oxygen to the muscles. All of this triggered by emotions affecting the autonomic nervous system and setting us into the "fight or flight" response. Interestingly, the adrenal gland which releases epinephrine when triggered by increased emotions happens to be the only organ in the entire body that has a direct link to the sympathetic branch of the autonomic nervous system. It is activated by emotions, and has powerful effects on the body. These same emotions can trigger powerful effects with the conscious singularity and invoke Higgs boson particles. allowing them to manifest and interact with our physical world. Most often, it is some type of apparition, shadow or mist that is witnessed, or in rare cases even photographed. We need to keep in mind that for anything to be seen or captured with a camera photons have to physically bounce off of it and reflect back to our eye, or imaging device. This cannot happen unless the object being seen or photographed has at least some amount of physical mass at the time of observation or imaging. It's important to realize this because this kind of interaction is only possible if the object has some amount of mass. Interestingly, in many cases an apparition is caught on film that had not been seen by the human eye. This is likely due to the momentary increase in photon intensity from the camera flash. Intensity does not refer to the strength of the light, but the number of photons. In regular ambient light the intensity is fairly steady and there may not be enough photons reflecting off an anomaly with low mass to be seen. It's only when a sudden spike in intensity occurs from a flash that there are just enough reflected back to be caught in that split second of exposure and captured on film. The figures on the following pages include some of the more credible photographs taken, starting with recognizable apparitions.

Full Apparitions

In Figure 2.1 you can see an apparition behind the officer in the top row, fourth in from the left. This photograph was taken in 1919, and first published in 1975 by Sir Victor Goddard, a retired R.A.F. officer. The photo was of Goddard's squadron who had served at the HMS Daedalus training facility in England during World War I. They posed for a last group photo before being disbanded after the war ended. The apparition seen behind the fourth officer in the top row is said to be Freddy Jackson, an air mechanic who was accidentally killed by an airplane propeller two days earlier. Members of the squadron recognized him immediately in the photo. His funeral took place the same day this photograph was taken. There is some argument as to the exact cause of his death, and whether he served as an airman or artilleryman, but records confirm that Frederick William Jackson did die around the time this photograph was taken.

Figure 2.1 Fredrick Jackson, top back row, fifth in from the left

Interestingly, the face of the apparition has areas of light reflection and shadow at the same angle as the rest of the photo, which means the ambient light is reflecting off of it as if it is striking something real with mass. This supports the temporary mass to consciousness through Higgs boson interaction theory.

Another example of an apparition is seen in Figure 2.2. This is a photograph of Combermere Abbey library which was taken in 1891 by Sybel Corbet. On the left you can clearly see a form sitting in the chair. It is believed to be the ghost of Lord Combermere, a British cavalry commander from the early 1800s. He died in 1891. His funeral was taking place at the same time this photograph was taken. Again, we can see the ambient light of the room reflecting off of the entities right side. Light photons coming in from the window on the left, striking something with some amount of mass and reflecting back to the camera.

Figure 2.2 Lord Combermere, sitting in a chair to the left

Coincidentally, both Lord Combermere and Fredrick Jackson had suffered traumatic deaths just days before these photos were taken. Jackson reportedly was killed by a spinning airplane propeller; Lord Combermere was struck in the road and killed by a horse and carriage. Both appear in these photos at the time of their funerals, apparently unaware that they had died. As stated before, the conscious is unaware it is dead, and just continues about what seems a normal routine to them, the same as when a person is asleep and dreaming, unaware that they are.

It seems many of those who experienced a violent death end up lingering unknowingly. One other example of this was a non-visible manifestation in the form of an EVP recorded in Fairland Indiana. Allegheny Airlines flight 853 had a mid air collision and crashed there in 1969. The plane was carrying 78 passenger and 4 crew members. The other plane was being flown by a student pilot. Everyone involved was killed in the crash. Two paranormal investigators from Daywalkers Paranormal group visited the site in 2012 and recorded several EVPs, including one that said "Did we crash?" And another that said "Maybe he doesn't know he's dead".

Figure 2.3 Allegheny crash site, Fairland, Indiana

Another rather famous apparition with a long history of sightings dating back 180 years is the Brown Lady of Raynham Hall, in Figure 2.4. Raynham Hall is a country house in Norfolk, England that has stood for nearly 400 years. The ghost is said to be that of Lady Dorothy Walpole, sister of Robert Walpole, the first Prime Minister of Great Britain. She was married to Lord Charles Townsend (a British statesman), and died in the house in 1726 from smallpox. The first recording sighting of her was by Lucia C. Stone in 1835, when Lord Townsend had invited some guests to the Hall for Christmas. Colonel Loftus and another guest both reported seeing her approaching their bedrooms. Colonel

Loftus said upon seeing her, he was drawn to her dark, empty eye sockets. His sighting scared some of the staff so much that they resigned and left Raynham Hall permanently.

The next reported sighting came one year later in 1836 by Captain Frederick Marryat, a friend of the novelist Charles Dickens. He was a British Royal Navy officer, and did not believe what he had heard. He had a theory that the stories of the ghost were due to local smugglers trying to keep people away from the area. He brought a revolver with him, and requested to stay a night in the haunted room to prove his theory. She had often been seen in this room, and a portrait of her hung on the wall. He slept in the room each night with the loaded gun under his pillow. The first two nights he saw nothing. On the third night, while he was getting ready for bed, two young men (nephews of the baronet) knocked on his door and asked him to come down the corridor to their room to give his opinion on a new gun just arrived from London. He was dressed informally "in just his shirt and trousers", but since it was late and they were the only three still up, he agreed to go, taking his revolver with him. After inspecting the new gun and talking with the men, he decided to return down the dark corridor back to his room. The two men accompanied him back. On their way, they saw a faint glow of something like a lamp coming toward them from the other end of the corridor. One of the men whispered that it was "One of the ladies going to visit the nurseries". The bedroom doors in that corridor faced each other, and each room had a double door with a space between. Because Captain Marryat was dressed in a manner that would have been considered informally inappropriate, he ducked into one of the bedrooms and closed the double doors, peering through the space between the doors, waiting for the young lady to pass. The other two men did the same in another empty room. As Captain Marryat watched through the crack in the door, the light became brighter as the woman approached closer passing down the corridor. As she passed, he recognized her face immediately as the woman in the portrait of his room, the Brown Lady. With his finger on the trigger of his revolver, he was about to demand it stop and give the reason for its presence there. That's when it stopped on its own right at the door he was behind and turned toward him with a malicious grin. Captain Marryat sprang into the corridor and fired his revolver directly at her face. She instantly disappeared. The bullet passed through the outer door of the room on the opposite side of the corridor, and lodged in the panel of the inner one. All three men witness this event.

In 1936 the apparition was witnessed again, but this

time caught on film by Captain Hubert C. Provand and Indre Shira. Provand had his head under a black cloth on the back of a camera they had set up facing the staircase on the first floor. His colleague, Indre Shira was standing near him holding the flashgun for the camera. Suddenly he yelled to Provand "Quick! quick! There's something! Are you ready?" Provand replied 'yes' and opened the camera shutter. Shira fired the flashgun. A few seconds later Provand came out from under the cloth and asked Shira what he was so excited about, as he had not seen anything through the camera while under the cloth. Shira said he saw a figure start to form on the staircase and slowly descend down it. Provand didn't believe him and promptly bet him five pounds that there would be nothing on the photographic plate when they developed it.

Later they left to go develop the picture. When they were back in their darkroom together developing the plate, they were amazed to see an image of the ghost form on the photographic plate of the staircase. Shira was so excited he ran down to get chemist Benjamin Jones to witness the image developing. Jones later signed a declaration stating that he did witness the image of the ghost forming in the photograph during the developing process. Several experts, including Harry Price, have since declared the photograph to also be genuine. The photograph was published in Country Living magazine in England in 1936, and in Life magazine in the United States in 1937.

Courtesy of Fortean Picture Library

Figure 2.4 The Brown Lady of Raynham Hall, Norfolk, England

Shadow Figures

Shadow figures are the result of particles shifted 180 degrees out of phase with the light photons striking them. So far we have discussed the visible ghost manifestations resulting from increased or neutral emotional states. If the emotional state is neutral, or melancholic, then the Higgs is not invoked, no mass is conveyed to the conscious singularity, and we see nothing. If the emotional state is increased or decreased, not neutral, we do see something, either an abstract mist or recognizable form (depending on the level of subconscious) as in the previous examples. We are able to see these because ambient light photons striking these temporarily mass-bound particles are reflected back to our eyes or cameras. However, sometimes manifestations show themselves as shadows only.

Shadows are the result of a lack of photons being reflected back to our eye (or recording device), which means that when we see a manifestation as a shadow, light photons striking it are not being reflected, but are actually being absorbed by the entity. This is caused again by the emotion state, not in an increased or neutral state, but in a negative state. When the emotional state is that of depression or sadness, some of the particles comprising a conscious singularity undergo a phase shift. The laws of particle physics tell us that when a particle is shifted 180 degrees out of phase with the photons of light in the room striking it, the light is absorbed instead of reflected, and the result is a darkened or shadowed area. Not all of the light photons striking it will be out of phase, so it appears dark, but transparent. If all of the photons interacting with the manifestation were exactly 180 degrees out of phase, then the manifestation would appear as a solid black object, rather than a transparent shadow, (not to be confused with photon dispersion or blackbody radiation).

This explains shadow figures, as well as cold spots that can be felt or seen on thermal imaging. Photons make up not only visible light, but also heat, which is at the infrared end of the electromagnetic spectrum. When those photons are absorbed, there is a loss of heat, which results in a local temperature drop that can be either felt, or seen with a thermal imager.

Figure 2.5 shows an image of a shadow manifestation that was taken on the RMS Queen Mary. Originally built in Scotland, the Queen Mary was an ocean liner that sailed the North Atlantic Ocean from 1936 to 1967 for the Cunard White-Star Line. The primary voyages were between the United States and Europe. When World War II broke out, it was converted to a troopship and used for the duration of the war. When the war ended, the ship was refitted for passenger service. Retired from service in 1967, it is now permanently moored at the port in Long Beach, California, where it serves as a tourist attraction, with a restaurant and hotel. It has a long history of civilian and military passengers, and many sightings have taken place on the ship.

It is interesting to note that the shadow apparition in Figure 2.1 is only partially manifest from the legs down. As stated earlier, the level of subconscious self image is important because it affects the detail of self projection in the manifestation. A less self aware subconscious produces a less detailed self projection. In this case, very little manifestation of the lower extremities, likely because there is usually less focus on the legs and feet in the subconscious.

Figure 2.5 Shadow manifestation, RMS Queen Mary

This phenomenon can also occur with other parts of the body during a partial manifestation. For example, in Figure 2.6 an image of a headless shadow was captured walking through an empty room of an abandon school building in Iraq. In addition to missing the head, the body and legs are also somewhat transparent, and do not appear solid at all.

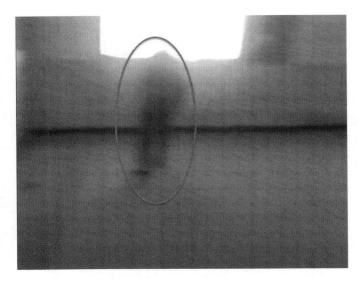

Figure 2.6 Shadow manifestation, abandon school, Iraq

It is remarkable to consider that ghosts actually do follow some of the basic rules of the physical world. For example, they have been seen walking upon a floors instead of sinking through them, or walking up and down stair cases. Although in some instances they do not follow the basic rules of physics and are seen floating stationary or moving. This is likely attributed to the subconscious again being less aware and not producing a full self projection. Recall that they are in somewhat of a dream state, and so may not be paying any attention to certain aspects of themselves. For example, how often you look down at, or even think about your own feet in dreams? The answer for you is liable to be rarely or never, so why should they? It is just human nature.

In contrast to full form apparitions and shadows, manifestations can also be abstract, such as the formless shadow image in Figure 2.7. In the foreground are some local tourists posing for a picture. Behind them, on the stone steps is an abstract shadow manifestation. This photograph was taken at Lawang Sewu, in Semarang, Indonesia.

Figure 2.7 Abstract shadow manifestation, Lawang Sewu, Indonesia

Lawang Sewu (meaning Thousand Doors) was built in 1904 and was originally used as a railway company in the Dutch East Indies. After the Japanese invaded Indonesia in 1942, the Japanese army took over Lawang Sewu. The basement of B building was turned into a prison, and several executions took place there. When Semarang was retaken by the Dutch in the battle of Semarang in October 1945, the Dutch forces used the tunnel leading into A building to sneak into the city. A battle followed and many Indonesian fighters were killed. Five employees working there were also killed. In addition to these deaths, a suicide also took place there.

Lawang Sewu (Figure 2.8) is said to be haunted, and many tourists visit there in hopes of seeing a ghost.

Figure 2.8 Lawang Sewu, Semarang, Indonesia

The Semarang city government, however, wants to make it an area for more social and cultural activities, and is trying to eliminate the buildings' reputation of being haunted. There are future plans for renovation of B building, which include office spaces, a food court and even a gym, but to many who live there, it will always be remembered for its alleged hauntings and violent history.

Figure 2.9 Lawang Sewu basement, the site of several executions and a suicide

Amorphic Mists

Perhaps without the physical scaffold of the living brain, entangled energy particles of the conscious singularity lack organized structure causing it to be in a dream state. If the conscious singularity is in a dream state with an unaware subconscious, the self projection will be diffuse and unorganized. In this case, combined with an increased or decreased but not neutral emotional state, the entity will manifest as an amorphic mist, such as the ones seen in Figures 2.10 and 2.11. These were photographed at Sachs Bridge. The bridge was built in 1854 and sits over Marsh Creek between Cumberland and Freedom Townships, in Adams County Pennsylvania. Both the Union and Confederate Armies used the bridge during the American Civil War in the Battle of Gettysburg. It is believed that three Confederate soldiers, one each from Kentucky, Tennessee and Virginia were convicted as Union spies and were hanged at the covered crossing in 1863 as the troops of General Robert E. Lee were withdrawing from the battlefield. There was also a post battlefield hospital set up near the bridge and many died there as well. The Battle of Gettysburg lasted only three days, but had over 46,000 casualties.

Figure 2.10 Amorphic mist, Sachs Bridge, Gettysburg, Pennsylvania

Figure 2.11 amorphic mist, Sachs Bridge, Gettysburg, Pennsylvania

3 NON-VISIBLE MANIFESTATIONS

Audible

In addition to apparitions, shadows and mists, there are also other non-visible forms of manifestation. These include such things as audible sounds, temperature variations, unexplained scents or odors, and physical contact events. Many people report hearing a voice, or footsteps. In some instances they have been captured on recording devices. EVP stands for electronic voice phenomena. It is when sounds, particularly voices of the dead are allegedly captured on electronic recording devices. As explained above, visible apparitions are seen because light photons are reflecting off of an entity that has temporarily gained partial mass through the Higgs boson force carrier. With EVPs, we also see force carriers at work. In this case it is not the Higgs, but another force carrier known in quantum physics as a phonon. Sound in the living world is generated by compression waves in the air. Phonons are force carriers that not only carry compression waves through solid matter, but now recently discovered, through the air as well. The devices being used in this field of physics research have been called 'sound lasers', or more accurately, phonon laser devices. This helps us understand how EVPs may be captured by microphone recording devices.

In addition to phonons, photons are also force carriers of electromagnetic forces. Depending on their energy level, photons also form radio waves, which can be received and recorded by electronic recording devices. When these photons emanate from a ghost, they can be picked up by nearby receivers and can be recorded and played back as an EVP.

However, it is important to keep in mind that much of the EVPs people capture end up being misinterpreted background noises, or voices from field investigators. Some sounds, although clearly audible and recorded by multiple recorders in the area at the time of recording, may not noticed by operators simply because they didn't appear to be voices. Such noise may only sound more 'voice-like' when subject to intense examination later, when the recording is reviewed. I personally listened to an EVP that was recorded during a paranormal investigation. At first it actually sounded like a voice whispering something inaudible. But after the recording was reviewed, it was determined to be the sound of one of the investigators shifting uncomfortably in a wooden chair after sitting in the same location for a long period of time waiting to catch something on tape. The sounds were actually of the person's clothing rubbing and a slight and quiet squeak noise made by the wooden chair itself.

Often times when investigators are listening to the playback recordings of EVPs they are expecting to hear something paranormal and are at risk for misinterpretation of the recorded noises because of psychological suggestion. This causes the person listening to misinterpret a noise as a voice actually saying something. You may have heard EVP recordings before, and most likely you were told before actually hearing it, or immediately after hearing it what was said by the "ghost". This power of suggestion in a way forces the listener's brain to hear the words suggested. It is actually best practice not to read or listen to another person's interpretation of what the recording allegedly says before hearing it, but to make your own decision after hearing it. Try it next time you are presented with an EVP and you will likely only hear noise, or something that could be any of a combination of words. The same EVP can usually be interpreted to say completely different words when listened to by different people without pre-suggestion.

This is not to discount EVPs entirely. A few of them have provided actual and clearly heard words, which, at the time of their recordings did not have an identifiable source. However, there are many examples available to listen to and judge for yourself online. Unfortunately, the majority of them are hard to discern as actual words, if any, when you eliminate other peoples' suggestions and interpretations. You should just simply listen to it without bias and try to decide on your own if you actually hear something real or relevant. One good resource that has a lot of science based information, including EVP recording samples, is the Association for the Scientific Study of Anomalous Phenomena, based in the United Kingdom. They can be found easily online, and have a lot of good information related to real scientific studies.

If you are trying to capture an EVP, bear in mind a few things to avoid. Sound recorders can also pick up mechanical tape movements in analogue recorders, objects brushing against the recorder (or something it is attached to) or the wind or draughts blowing across the microphone. Therefore, you should not hold the device while recording.

Olfactory

Unexplained fragrances or odors are another type of non-visible manifestation. Scientifically, to smell something you have to have odorant molecules. These molecules hover in the air and pass into your nose to contact microscopic hair like extensions on specialized epithelial cells in the nose. These cells propagate a signal to the dendrites on the neurons that compose the olfactory nerve, the nerve that senses smells and sends those odor signals to the brain. The olfactory nerve is also the first cranial nerve extending from the brain. It is a scientific fact that smell has the strongest effect on invoking memories. You may have even experienced this yourself, if you've ever smelled something that took you back to a particular time or place and reminded you of old memories.

There have been cases of people reporting smelling odors with no traceable source. I have personally experienced this myself, and now hope to shed some light on it. In my case, it occurred during the winter months several years ago. I was in the living room of the old house I grew up in, along with my sister and my mother. It was very cold outside, and there were no flowers or other such vegetation growing at

that time of the year. The windows were all closed
and we did not have any flowers in the house. We
had been sitting in the living room watching TV
when suddenly all three of us could smell lilacs. My
mother was the first to ask "Can you smell that?
What is it?" Both my sister and I could also smell it.
I said "it smells like flowers", to which my mother
replied "yeah, lilacs". Then she said "Where is it
coming from?" None of us had an answer. It was
very pleasant and smelled as if there were fresh lilacs
in the room. It persisted for a few more seconds and
then suddenly it was gone. This happened in the
same house two more times. The last time it
occurred with me the scent was floral, but this time
roses. I remember it vividly, the smell was so strong
and sweet, but that occurrence only lasted about four
seconds, then vanished. Until this day, my family
members and I have had no explanation of what
caused this. Obviously it was not an olfactory
illusion because all three of us smelled it at the same
time, and smelled the same thing. Yet there was no
traceable source, no flowers inside, none growing
outside, no one else in the house; and with the
windows sealed for the winter, no chance of what we
had smelled coming from a source outside of the
house. So what was it?

The only scientific explanation is that there were
odorant molecules present, which we were all able to

detect. But where did they come from? The answer goes back to the Higgs boson particle and the elements that govern manifestation. In the living, memories and emotions are tightly linked and controlled by the limbic system in the brain. When the patterned quantum vibrations that comprise consciousness leave the body at the time of death, they take with them the conscious and pre/subconscious which contain memories and emotion. If the emotions of a conscious singularity can reach a certain state, something will manifest - this is when the Higgs boson is invoked and conveys mass to particles, atoms and molecules. In this case it would be odorant molecules, reproduced from the entity's memory. Just as clothing, for example a green striped dress or military uniform, is reproduced from subconscious memory and self projection when we see a full and recognizable apparition. Inanimate objects such as a person's clothes, a soldier's gun or even the smell of flowers can manifest if those things are projected by an entity's subconscious and given temporary partial mass by the Higgs boson, allowing us to see, hear, touch or even smell something temporarily. Of course the Higgs persists in this instance only momentarily, and then returns all mass from those particles, atoms and molecules back to the Higgs field, causing the manifestation to vanish. So we are able to see something, or even smell something but only momentarily.

Tactile

Physical interactions are another non-visible manifestation. Just as bursts of adrenaline inducing emotions invoke sudden and dramatic changes in a living body; they also invoke bursts of other sudden force carriers in the nonliving. Force carriers such as phonons and/or gravitons which can directly impact solid matter in our world, causing sounds to be heard, or items to be touched or moved. If something is touched or moved, it involves kinetic energy. When the mass temporarily conveyed to a ghost is combined with its inherent energy, the result is mass particles with stored energy which can be translated into moving energy, or in other words kinetic energy. For example, if you are holding a ball in your hand, the ball has mass, but no energy imparted to it. It just exists there sitting in your hand doing nothing. However, if you were to throw the ball, your hand would be imparting energy to an object with mass (in this case the ball), which would leave your hand and fly across the room. You caused some of the moving energy from your arm and hand to be transferred to the ball, resulting in it having kinetic energy. The more energy you transfer to it, the stronger the kinetic force.

Kinetic energy from a ghost that has obtained some mass through the Higgs particle can be transferred in the same way to objects or people in the living world. Even if no mass is conveyed, and the entity remains invisible, it can still obtain and transfer kinetic energy. This is because the Higgs, like the photon, is a boson force carrier; and like the photon, also exhibits wave-particle duality. This means they can act as both matter and energy.

In physics, this is expressed by the formula:

$$p = h / \lambda = mc$$

where p is momentum, h is Planck's constant (a measurement of action in quantum mechanics), lambda (the upside down 'y' symbol) λ is the measure of wavelength, m is mass, and c is the speed of light in vacuum. This expression proves the wave–particle duality.

Not only does it convey mass, but also carries kinetic force. (It's important here to note that momentum is not the same thing as kinetic energy. Momentum is a vector quantity; while kinetic energy is a scalar quantity. Recall that the Higgs boson is a scalar particle force carrier). Because of this, an entity can remain unseen without mass, but still have the ability to transfer kinetic energy and move objects, or even touch or push people.

This mode of interaction was, in fact, my first type of unexplained experience. I was in my early twenties, and at that time was often in the habit of wearing a baseball cap. One day while wearing my hat, I got into my car in the driveway of our old house where we grew up. The house we lived in was very old. In fact, my sister traced it all the way back to the 1700s through county tax records. (At one time it had even served as a doctor's office.) My sister was always more sensitive to paranormal events than I was; and I simply thought she was just imagining it when she said she could see or sense things. I never really paid attention or gave much consideration to those kinds of things, until the day I had my tactile experience. I got in my car, shut the door and got ready to turn the key. Suddenly something sharply tapped the visor of my hat. It was as if someone had flicked it with their finger. I did not image this. I heard the 'tap' noise, I felt the hat move and I saw the visor jump downward slightly. At first I thought something fell on my hat, but I was in the car, and the ceiling was less than three inches above my head, so nothing could have fallen on me. Regardless of that, I looked up at the ceiling and saw nothing. I then took my hat off and checked to see if there was something on it; there was nothing there either. I was truly baffled and sat there for a few minutes trying to figure out what had just transpired. This incident happened to me three more times after that in the same way, spread out over about one year's time; and occurred in two different vehicles, parked in the same driveway. I was astonished at this and for years had no rational explanation for it. It was the first thing that began to open my mind to even consider paranormal events. After years of science courses, and doing research, I believe it was due to a tactile interaction of some kind.

What about passing through matter, such as walls? We now know this is possible due to the OSQAR experiment at CERN. OSQAR stand for the Optical Search for QED Vacuum Bifringence, Axion and Photon Regeneration. The experiment is known to physicists as "Light shining through a wall". In the experiment, the researchers direct a laser light at a wall. Before the laser hits the wall, it passes through a nine tesla magnetic field, which converts some of the photons in the beam into a axions, a newly discovered type of particle, which can then pass through the wall and emerge on the other side again as light in the form of detectable photons. Under the right conditions, the laser undergoes a conversion and can pass right through a solid wall, re-emerging on the other side.

The quantum vibrations that take on mass via the

Higgs particle can form the apparition, but when it encounters something like a wall in its path, its subconscious changes to alter its physical properties, losing mass back to the Higgs field so that it may pass through the wall as a type of energy only, perhaps as axions, and emerge on the other side, continuing uninterrupted on its desired path. So their existence still follows the laws of conservation where mass is converted back to energy via the force carrier Higgs.

If their existence follows the laws of conservation, then they must also follow some of the other laws governing particle physics, meaning they can also see us, and hear us. Reflected light and compression sound waves are carried by force carriers, to which they have an accessible link. Light photons are force carriers and reflect off of us and other solid matter. Compression sound waves in air when we talk or make noise are carried through the air by force carriers as well. Their link to force carriers is constant. Photons interact with them all the time, not only in the standard classical/physical model as it does with us - light bounces off of a physical object and into our eyes, but also in a massless energy model. Again, this is because of the wave-particle duality that photons have been recently proven to exhibit. They can act as both matter and energy.

Because of their energy duality, they can interact with ghosts as well us, even though we both exist in seemingly separate planes at times. Until now, wave-particle duality was only a theory, and photon interaction did not always make sense in scientific terms, because we had not yet discovered its true nature. Albert Einstein wrote: "It seems as though we must use sometimes the one theory and sometimes the other, while at times we may use either. We are faced with a new kind of difficulty. We have two contradictory pictures of reality; separately neither of them fully explains the phenomena of light, but together they do". The same is true for what we know about paranormal phenomena; ghosts and their interactions with our world. Although they do not have physical bodies, they can still interact with us. For example, they can see us and our surroundings. Ghosts lack the physical limitations of the human body, and therefore are likely sensitive not only the visible light wave lengths of the electromagnetic spectrum, but to the other ends of the spectrum as well, such as infrared, which would allow them to see in the dark. This explains why they are equally active in light or dark. Another form of electromagnetic force is also thermal energy, which can be detected by infrared sensors and recorded.

4 FALSE POSITIVES

It is important to approach all potential observations in a scientific manner to avoid 'false positives'. In other words, focus on factual evidence in seeking the truth regarding an observation. There are many photographs of 'ghosts', but it's essential to realize not all photographs of alleged apparitions are real. Sometimes they are purposely faked, while other times they are the results of mistakes or lack of knowledge. 'Orbs' are a good example.

Orbs are circles of light with white to grey color that appear sometimes in photographs. Despite overwhelming evidence that orbs are simply photographic artifacts, many people still believe in them. The artifacts are formed when dust particles (or sometimes moisture droplets) in front of the camera lens are captured out of focus. Because they are out of focus, their highlights form a circular pattern, as seen in Figure 4.1.

Figure 4.1 Photo of alleged orbs, usually dust, moisture or pollen reflecting camera flash

Before digital cameras, orbs were never heard of, but suddenly became a popular phenomena when more and more people began using them. Now, as the technology has improved, less and less orbs are being reported. Professional photographers recognize and refer to orbs as "circles of confusion" - a technical term used in the field of photography. If you look at the following photograph of a tree out of focus, you will see many points of light becoming circular and forming overlapping orbs.

Figure 4.2 Out of focus tree showing orbs

The reason they are became so prevalent with early digital cameras is due to the fact that the sensor chips in the cameras were physically smaller than a 35mm film frame. To compensate for this, wider-angle lenses were needed for digital cameras so they could show the same area of view in a frame as a 35mm film camera. The problem is wide-angle lenses change the depth of field. The depth of field is the area in front of the camera lens where objects are in focus. If an object is outside of this field either too close or too far from the lens, it will be captured out of focus, forming a circular highlight, Figure 4.3. These usually appear in the area where the flash is strong enough to illuminate tiny particles, like dust, water droplets or small insects, that are just too close to the camera to be in focus. Such objects produce expanded circles of confusion that appear as orbs. Because individual specs of dust are tiny, they only have a single highlight and so produce individual orbs. Some larger objects, like a small insect for example, may have several highlights and so produce multiple overlapping orbs.

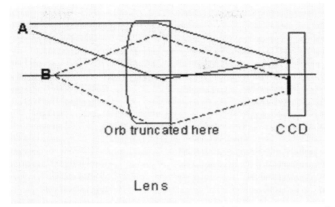

Figure 4.3 CCD camera sensor picks up truncated light rays forming an orb

Structural limitations have also plagued cameras before the digital era. The first commercially available Polaroid film camera came about back in 1948. Because the image is captured and developed onto the film right in the camera, it makes faking a Polaroid difficult to impossible, but an artifact can appear if there is a shutter problem. Figure 4.4 shows a Polaroid that was taken in 1968 with a supposed apparition captured.

Figure 4.4 Polaroid showing alleged apparition

The man in the picture is author Robert A. Ferguson, giving a speech at a spiritualist convention in Los Angeles, California on psychic telemetry. Standing next to him is what appears to be a faint apparition, which he later identified as his brother, Walter

Ferguson, who died in 1944 during World War II. Unfortunately, if you look closely at the details of the alleged apparition, you will notice strong evidence that this was a simple case of a double exposure. Aside from the fact that the 'apparition' and Mr. Ferguson look exactly identical, are the same height, with same facial features lining up at the same level, and both leaning at nearly the same angle, they are also dressed exactly alike. The 'apparition' appears much darker because of the limited time of the double exposure that caused this ghosting artifact. The final giveaway is the tie. The pattern is also exactly the same, dark with light stripe in the middle at the same spot and angle. If you look closely at the tie the 'ghost' is wearing, it is the same tie, difficult to see because it is darker, but the pattern is there. This photograph was likely the result of an innocent accidental double exposure which everyone, including Mr. Ferguson, mistook in wishful thinking for something else.

As mentioned earlier, some EVPs are also misinterpretations. Often times they are inaudible and are assigned a meaning by those anxious to hear the voice of a ghost. The power of suggestion then causes others subsequently listening to the recording to hear what they are told it is saying before they even hear it, which causes them to believe it too. EVPs need to be clear, and identified separately from other possible artifacts, or voices of the living in close proximity to the recording device.

Although EMF/K2 meters have gained great popularity in recent years, they too are not infallible and end up detecting electromagnetic fields emanating from normal sources. Such common sources include power outlets, normal electrical wiring in walls, circuit boxes, metal plumbing (which can carry current), wireless devices, cell phones, wifi routers, cell towers, cordless phones, etc. Additionally, the readings may become inaccurate if they are used in a larger building with 3-phase wiring, or if there is some separate electrical equipment wired in 3-phase near single phase wired equipment. In this case, even though the equipment is not on the same circuit, the electromagnetic fields they produce can overlap and cause paradoxical readings on an EMF meter. Because they are out of phase with each other, there are anomalous drops in the readings that normally wouldn't appear.

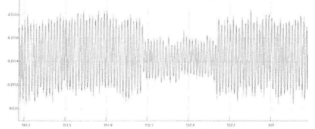

Figure 4.5 Magnetometer reading showing 3-phase interference from building wiring

Another problem is not taking normal variations over time in EM fields into consideration when measuring a baseline. If the time period for a baseline taken is too short, then it becomes useless because normal variations that occur after the short sample will appear to be abnormal. Figure 4.6 below shows all the normal variations taken within a ten minute period. To get a true baseline, a much longer time should be used.

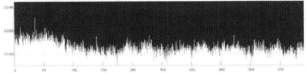

Figure 4.6 Electromagnetic baseline over a 10 minute period

There is also the problem of EIFs - varying magnetic fields that can cause hallucinations in some people. EMF meters cannot detect these fields because they aren't sensitive enough and can't distinguish between frequencies. Unfortunately, 3-phase interference, EIFs and inaccurate baseline readings along with stray EM fields make EMF meters an ineffective tool in paranormal investigations.

Another misconception many people have is using a metal flashlight as a type of detector to speak to spirits. It was first done when investigators switched a flashlight on, then turned the back cap just until the light went out. They proceeded to ask any ghosts present questions and the flashlight began turning itself on and off. It has since been discovered that this happened because of the expansion and contraction on the internal parts of the flashlight from heat generated by the incandescent bulb. When the parts expand and contract, they open and close an electrical circuit with the batteries causing the light to flicker off and on by itself.

Moving doors are another event some people have reported. Doors rattling, opening or closing on their own may be the result of paranormal event, or may not. Often times this is not a ghost, but actually caused by something in physics known Bernoulli's principle and the Venturi effect, and can occur in any room with a fireplace. Wind moving over the roof outside flowing across the top opening of the chimney causes a low pressure to form inside the flue and create a small amount of vacuum at the entrance of the fireplace. Air is then drawn up the chimney through the fireplace. This creates a slightly lower air pressure in the room, which pulls air from adjacent rooms through the entering doorways. If the pressure is low enough, the airflow into the room with the fireplace can cause a door to close, or open depending on the direction of the hinges. Figure 4.7 illustrates this.

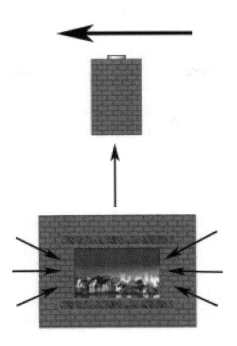

Figure 4.7 Fireplace updraft causing negative air pressure in a room

The Venturi effect explains that as air passes through a restriction (in this case the chimney), the velocity increases, causing a decrease in air pressure (in the room). An equation for the drop in pressure due to the Venturi effect is derived from a combination of two other laws in physics: Bernoulli's principle and the Continuity equation, and is expressed as follows:

$$p_1 - p_2 = P/2 \left(v^2_2 - v^2_1 \right)$$

No spirits involved, just simple physics.

Several years ago, there was a general misconception that "auras" could be photographed using a technique called kerlian photography. Despite the subsequent scientific explanation of how it actually works, people still continued to believe what they were seeing were images of the actual aura or life-force caught on film. Kerlian photography was developed in 1939, but didn't become publicized until 1970. The photographs show a glowing aura around objects that are photographed. In Figure 4.8, a kerlian photograph shows the complete aura of a leaf whose top part has been cut off.

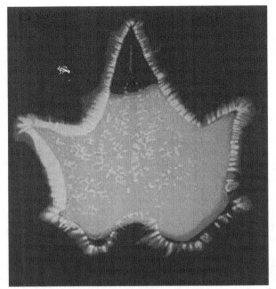

Figure 4.8 Kerlian photograph of a torn leaf

Even though part of the leaf is missing, the entire outline is still present. It looks convincing at first, but this is unfortunately another example of a 'false positive'. The process of taking a Kirlian photo is actually very simple and does not even require a camera. First, a sheet of photographic film is placed on top of a metal plate. Next, the object to be photographed is placed on top of the film. High voltage current is then applied to the metal plate to create the exposure. The electrical coronal discharge between the object and the metal plate is captured on the film. It results in a glowing "life-force aura" around the photographed object once the film is developed. What we are actually seeing is simply the remnants of electron discharge from the charge plate to the object on the film called a coronal plasma discharge. There is no life-force involved. In fact, any non-living object can also be photographed, as seen in Figure 4.9.

Figure 4.9 Kerlian photograph of a coin

Of course the use of technology is necessary if we wish to make new discoveries, but it should be used in the proper context to obtain reliable scientific results.

.

5 TOOLS

Detection is the key in discovering anything in the fields of science. It was the detectors at CERN that discovered the Higgs, and other never before seen particles, and it continues to do so now and into the future. In looking for evidence of ghosts, it is necessary to use the same scientific methodology. There are many types of detection tools currently in use. But they only detect in limited fields. I propose looking in a new direction based on my theory of temporary transient mass transfer.

Current Devices

Currently, there are many different tools that paranormal investigators use to try and detect ghosts. Unfortunately, conventional equipment is expensive, and offers only limited results. Still, there has occasionally been some good evidence recorded. One of the most popular tools in use is, of course, the video camera. Also available are various lighting devices. In addition to recording in regular, ambient light, they also use night vision and full spectrum lighting to potentially catch something anomalous. The full spectrum includes not only the normal range of visible white light, but also in the infra red and ultra violet ends. For the infra red end, FLIR thermal cameras have become very popular. They show a picture of the environment as a thermal image, thus allowing hot and cold spots to be seen. It may be worth repeating that high photon intensity may increase the chances of catching an image during exposure. Perhaps there is s certain threshold of intensity that is needed to achieve enough reflection for an image to form. In this case, an experiment with a variable intensity strobe type flash could result in capturing an image.

Aside from imaging, catching something on an audio device is also popular. There are a few types of these devices being used. One type is called a "ghost box", and matches electromagnetic and temperature changes in the environment to preselected words from a built in data base to form sentences. Although the accuracy of this has not been confirmed to provide any useful information. Another device in use is called a "spirit box" and uses radio frequency sweeps to generate white noise over which the user hopes to catch an EVP. This device is prone to detecting unwanted radio waves and, unfortunately, often times the resulting EVPs are unclear and difficult to determine what, if anything, is being said.

EMF/K2 meters as mentioned above are also popular. Again, they alert the user to changes in electromagnetic fields. Many people involved with paranormal investigating believe ghosts have the ability to manipulate or change these fields. But electromagnetic fields are produced by anything with an electric current, and it is normal for there to be fluctuations in an ordinary household current. So it could be difficult to discern what is actually causing any changes that may be picked up by the meter. MEL meters are also similar devices that measure temperature changes in the immediate environment, along with the electromagnetic fields. Other temperature measuring devices are also available and are used to measure temperature and humidity changes as well.

Lasers have become another popular tool. They are used to project an array of dots of laser light over an area, usually set up in front of a camera. If anything passes through the field it is picked up on the camera. Another way they are used is to have them project a straight line grid over an area in conjunction with a camera. The grid set up allows for more information to be gathered, such as speed and possibly mass of an object moving through it. If accurate, this could provide useful information.

Motion sensors are sometimes employed to monitor empty rooms and signal a response if type of motion is picked up. There are two types of motion sensors: passive and active. Passive motion sensors detect changes in the infrared (heat) spectrum and signal when something emitting heat passes into its monitoring field. Active motion sensors actually send out ultrasonic waves that are reflected back to the sensor. If the pattern of the returning waves is disrupted by something passing through, an alarm is triggered, but most of these devices are usually not sensitive enough to detect what investigators are looking for.

Trigger props are another item. These are generally in the form of a stuffed animal that is used in hopes of gaining the attention of a child spirit. But these can also be used for other age groups as well, since animals don't correspond to any particular age or time period. They are readily recognizable and may actually invoke an emotional response.

Geophones are also used by some in an attempt to

detect things like footsteps. It is actually a vibration sensor and can be positioned on a surface to detect physical vibrations.

Other items such as Ion counters and Geiger counters have also seen use. Ion counters detect ionic changes in the air and the devices come in various sensitivities. Investigators are also sometimes plagued with unexplained equipment problems, such as quickly draining batteries, most likely the result of abnormal paramagnetic ion fields that draw out electrons. Perhaps a device to detect paramagnetic ions would be helpful in identifying abnormal anomalies.

Geiger counters are also sometimes used. These detect beta and gamma radiation, although other radiation detectors that can also pick up alpha and x-ray radiation are also available. Gauss meters and magnetometers are also used by some in search of paranormal phenomena.

Despite the vast array of items and equipment available, it seems difficult to obtain useful information. However, many strive to collect as much data as possible. The more information we gain, the closer we come to obtaining the evidence needed to support a theory.

New Gear

Since we now know about the Higgs boson and how it can impart mass, it may be useful to try detecting transient mass in a field of observation. There is a new device that has recently been developed called a QMD (Quantum Mass Detector) which can sense the presence of changes or manifestation of mass in a room. It is a new type of field disturbance sensor that uses quantum energy (photons) to detect the presence or change of mass in the field it is monitoring. This may be helpful in identifying any Higgs boson-particle interaction during a manifestation.

Figure 5.1 Quantum mass detector (from **ghostscience.org**)

There are a few other devices that may be worth mentioning. With the right modifications, they might provide some kind of useful information. One example is an actinometer. This is a device that is used to measure certain aspects of radiation and heat energy by measuring the intensity of photons. Bolometers, thermopiles, and photodiodes are also physical devices giving a reading that can be correlated to the number of photons detected. With more technical information and investigation, there may eventually be other devices developed that measure energy or particle fields and/or the four+ forces that govern particle physics themselves.

6 FIVE THEORIES

Reports of paranormal activity are not something recent. Though there has been little official scientific research on paranormal phenomena, people have been reporting such things for millennia. In fact, one of the oldest documented cases dates back nearly two thousand years. One of the first ever was reported in a letter written by a Roman named Gaius Plinius Caecilius Secundus, also known as Pliny the Younger. He was born in the year 61 AD and lived until 113 AD. He was a lawyer and magistrate of ancient Rome, and was considered by all to be an honest and moderate man. He wrote hundreds of letters to emperors and historians, which are of significant historical importance as they record the happenings from that time period.

In a letter to one of his patrons, Lucias Sura, he described a haunted villa in Athens. At the time, no one wanted to live in the villa because many said that it was haunted. As a result, it remained empty until the philosopher Athenodorus (c.74 BC – 7 AD) arrived in the city. He was unconcerned by the house's reputation and so moved in. That first night, an apparition of an old man bound in chains appeared and beckoned to him. The apparition vanished once it reached the courtyard, and Athenodrus carefully noted and marked the spot. The next morning he requested the magistrate have the spot dug up. There was found the skeleton of an old man bound with chains. After the skeleton was given a proper burial, the ghost never appeared again. (Figure 6.1)

Figure 6.1 Athenodorus witnesses the apparition.

Another ancient account is written in the Bible, in the first book of Samuel, where Saul sees and speaks with the ghost of Samuel. Saul was the first king of Israel and Judah, who was anointed by the prophet Samuel. Later, after Samuel dies, Saul goes to speak with the witch of Endor who summons Samuel from the grave. Saul asks him what will happen when his army goes to battle with the philistines at Gilboa. Samuel tells him that he and his sons will all perish. In the battle, it's reported that Saul commits suicide to avoid capture; and that his three sons are also killed. All as predicted by the ghost of Samuel.

SAUL AND THE WITCH OF ENDOR
Then said the woman, Whom shall I bring up unto thee? And he said, Bring me up Samuel... (I Samuel 28:11)   (28, 7)

Figure 6.2 Saul sees and speaks with the ghost of Samuel

Over the years, many theories have developed. The first is that ghosts are the spirits of people who have died. Many religions have held and supported this belief. However, there is much debate as to where the spirit, or as I have defined it, conscious singularity, goes after death. Most Christian faiths believe in destinations designated as 'Heaven' or 'Hell'. Although unofficially many also believe it is possible for them to remain here on Earth. Some consider this a lesser type of punishment than 'Hell' and refer to it as 'Purgatory'. Perhaps these places are actually some of the extra dimensions science is searching for.

The second theory is that they are remnants of past events somehow recorded into the environment. This is often times referred to as residual hauntings. Some paranormal investigators believe this is the result of certain geologic rock formations or bodies of water underground that can by some means hold a faint recording of events. What bolsters this idea is the supposed recurrence of the same paranormal event in the same area. However, as stated before, a person that is deceased doesn't know they are dead, and their conscious singularity is in a dream state. Because of this they are prone to a dream state reality that often doesn't make sense for them, but they accept it regardless of this. One type of dream in the living that many people experience is a recurring dream. This is a situation in which they experience the same dream repeatedly for a long period of time. Often times these can be nightmarish or pleasant, depending on the individual and their past experiences or memories. If a conscious singularity is caught in a recurring dream state, they will unknowingly act out those experiences repeatedly over a long period of time, just the same as recurring dreams do in the living.

The third theory is that it all comes from the mind. This theory dismisses all possibility of paranormal activity and sums things up to simple hallucinations. Although, another avenue of thought on this also suggests that there might be some link to the subconscious being able to project things outside of the human mind and into the environment itself. Along that line of thinking is the implication that this may originate from either a single person's thoughts, or as a collective from a group of people.

The fourth theory refutes the idea that ghosts exist. It is more along the lines of religious beliefs. It is the idea that ghosts are really either demons attempting to harm or trick us; or angels that are here to protect us. Under this theory, there is inference that demons can portray other people in human form or even possess them; while angels are thought of as guardians of the living in contrast.

The fifth theory proposes that ghosts are interdimensional beings. This doesn't necessarily mean they are aliens. Instead, it relies on the theories of multiple dimensions. There is also the idea of an existing multiverse, composed of several parallel universes. The idea being that on occasion there is some type of temporary crossover that causes individuals from those places to cross into ours. Carrying that thought a bit further, one might also speculate that we have the same ability to cross temporarily into another dimension or parallel reality, which some people might describe as astral projection or lucid dreaming.

Extra dimensions are another area of interest in quantum physics, and are being test for, but even if found, there are still many more questions that need to be answered. Not quite the same as theory number five, extra dimensions are thought to be part of our universe here, but hidden from our current view. Scientists pose many questions about them. How does energy exist and behave in extra dimensional planes? Does time exist in those planes? How is gravity dispersed through them?

Concerning paranormal events, many people pose other questions regarding extra dimensions as well. Are these dimensions what some refer to as "Heaven", "Hell" or "Purgatory"? Where might ghosts exist, since pure energy is not limited to a single dimension? The answer is in one of two places, either here in our dimension (as undetectable energy), or in an extra dimension parallel to ours. Extra dimensions are not science fiction but real theoretical realms in the field of quantum physics. They are something that physicists are working on now. They have been predicted and theorized upon, although not yet discovered. There is indirect evidence that points to their existence. The presence of extra dimensions would answer fundamental questions in physics such as why the universe is expanding so much slower than it should, and why gravity is so much weaker a force than it should be. In 2003 scientists discovered that the universe is expanding at 1×10^{59} (that's actually a million billion billion billion billion billion billion) times slower than expected, which means we don't have the whole picture. There is also a discrepancy between the strength of electromagnetic fields and gravity. To give another example, a simple refrigerator magnet creates an electromagnetic force that is stronger than the gravitational pull exerted by our entire planet, which means there's something else out there we haven't discovered yet. One theory is that gravity is this weak because it is spread out over extra dimensions.

Researchers at CERN believe one way to test this

theory is to find evidence of heavier versions of standard particles, called Kaluza-Klein states. These are two other types of force carriers (called Z and W bosons) with masses one hundred times greater than normal, which could be created in the particle collider at high energies. If detected, they would prove the existence of extra dimensions.

There are several reasons for their possible existence, including Superstring theory. Superstring theory is a possible unified theory of all basic forces. But it requires a 10 dimensional space-time, or else bad quantum states that they call 'ghosts' with unphysical negative probabilities become part of the spectrum. Theoretical physicists believe these extra dimensions do exist, and would contain particles similar to ours, but with higher mass. The scientists at CERN have been working on this and are planning to run some experiments to possibly find such particles. If these particles are detected when the LHC is run at full power, it will confirm the existence of those theorized extra dimensions, and may answer part of our puzzle as to where ghosts actually exist or disappear to when they lose mass or energy. The way the LHC works is basically as a particle collider, crashing high speed particles into each other and annihilating them. When this happens all kinds of exotic particles are formed and detected in a symmetrical pattern. If there are any empty zones in the patterns of the high speed collisions, it will indicate gravitons escaping to another dimension. Another finding would be microscopic black holes which would decay in a fraction of a second, but produce a burst of an enormous number of particles, which would also confirm the existence of extra dimensions. As stated by CERN, "Finding more on any of these subjects would open the door to yet unknown possibilities."

7 REINCARNATION

In addition to the five theories above, there is also
the additional theory of reincarnation. The concept
of reincarnation is subscribed to worldwide and dates
back several millennia to 1,000 BC in India. It is a
hypothesis that has gained much attention by
researches in past years. The idea is that the spirit of
a person leaves the physical body after death, taking
with it memories and emotions, and later re-enter in
a new body, minus the previous memories. That
person then grows up and lives another lifetime of
events, unaware of their previous existence.
However, sometimes fragments of those memories
survive. In fact, over the years there have been
thousands of documented cases in which people
remember small bits of past lives.

Dr. Ian Stevenson was one of the first researchers to extensively investigate claims of those who remembered pieces of their past lives. He was originally from Canada, but later became a licensed psychiatrist in the United States. He was part of the faculty at University of Virginia School of Medicine for fifty years, and served as chair of the department of psychiatry from 1957 to 1967. Subsequently, he served as Professor of Psychiatry from 1967 to 2001, and Research Professor of Psychiatry from 2002 until his death in 2007. In total, he documented over two thousand five hundred cases, and published twelve books on the subject, becoming internationally recognized for his research. His investigations were compiled from thousands of individuals in different countries from all around the world.

In most documented cases, the memories are strongest in children before the age of ten. After that they begin to fade. Some believe this is because children are temporally closer to the "other side", having just entered, or re-entered our world recently. Dr. Stevenson travelled extensively both here in the United States, and abroad in other countries to interview such children. He systematically documented each child's statements and, amazingly, was able to identify the deceased person the child identified with. He also verified the facts of the deceased person's life that matched the child's memory. In his investigations, Dr. Stevenson searched for refuting evidence and alternative explanations for the reports, and believed that his strict methods ruled out all possible normal explanations for the child's memories. He was accompanied in many of his travels by Tom Shroder, a journalist and editor at *The Washington Post.* In the beginning, Shroder participated as an observer and a skeptic. However, as they progressed, Shroder found it increasingly difficult to reject the concept of reincarnation, and in fact later published a book entitled *Old Souls: The Scientific Search for Proof of Past Lives.*

Working also with Stevenson was Dr. Jim Tucker, medical director of the Child and Family Psychiatry Clinic, and Associate Professor of Psychiatry and Neurobehavioral Sciences at the University of Virginia School of Medicine. Dr. Tucker is a board certified child psychiatrist who has continued the research he and Dr. Stevenson carried out previously; and has published his own book entitled *Life Before Life: A Scientific Investigation of Children's Memories of Previous Lives*. He has studied most of his cases in the U.S. and found that in about 70% of the cases of past lives, the deceased died from an unnatural cause. This suggests that a traumatic death may be linked to the hypothesized survival of self through reincarnation. Within his investigations, he has found that there is specific period of time between death and apparent rebirth. It is, on average, sixteen months. In addition, there is an interesting correlation that unusual birth-marks might match fatal wounds suffered by the deceased; a finding also asserted by Dr. Stevenson in his early work.

Although critics have argued there is no material explanation for reincarnation, or the survival of self, Tucker believes that quantum mechanics may offer a mechanism by which memories and emotions could carry over from one life to another. As afore mentioned, the recent discovery of OOR (orchestrated objective reduction) would support this. In quantum physics, the act of observation has an effect on particle superposition in the brain (specifically the microtubules) and collapses wave equations (objective reduction). Tucker argues this could support that "self" (in other words the conscious) may not be merely a by-product of the brain, but rather a separate entity that impinges on matter. He believes that viewing "self" as a basic, nonmaterial part of the universe makes it possible to envision it continuing to exist after the death of the brain. He explains it with the analogy of a televisor and a television transmission. The two work together but are separate. The televisor is required to decode the signal, but it does not create the signal. In a similar way, the brain may be required for awareness to express itself, but may not be the source of awareness.

8 DREAM STATES & AWARENESS

Understanding dream states and levels of awareness, along with how the conscious reacts to them gives us greater insight into some paranormal interactions and behavior. Just as most people don't realize they are dreaming while they're asleep, most ghosts are trapped in dream states, unaware they are dead. However, sometimes it is possible to change this in both living and deceased subjects. Lucid dreaming is a primary example. Lucid dreaming occurs when the person who is asleep becomes aware in their dream that they are dreaming. A great deal of study and research has been done on lucid dreaming, and has given us interesting insight on how the mind works in a dream state. In a lucid dream, the dreamer has an opportunity to exercise some degree of control over their participation within the dream or manipulate their experiences in the dream environment. Lucid dreams are often realistic and vivid. Research has shown that people produce higher amounts of beta-1 frequency band, 13–19 Hz, brain wave activity during lucid dreams. This means there is an increased amount of activity in the parietal lobes, making lucid dreaming a conscious process.

Rapid eye movement (REM)

When a person is dreaming, the eyes move rapidly. It has been found that these eye movements match the direction the dreamer is looking in within their dreamscape. Subsequently, trained lucid dreamers are able to communicate with researchers while dreaming by using their eye movements as signals. These intentional eye movements by the dreaming subject are recorded by a device called an electrooculogram. Normally, when a person is dreaming, the prefrontal cortex is deactivated during REM sleep. This is an area of the brain where working memory occurs. If this area is somehow activated, the recognition of dreaming occurs. If not, the person continues in their dream unaware they are dreaming. In the same way, a ghost will continue wandering, unaware they are dead. It is only if they somehow become aware of their current state that they then gain more control over themselves and their actions and interactions. Without this awareness, they simply continue on unknowingly, with no perception of time. The same lack of time perception also occurs in the living during sleep. However, studies have shown time perception while counting during a lucid dream is about the same as during waking life. Lucid dreamers counted out ten seconds while dreaming, signaling the start and the end of the count with a pre-arranged eye signal measured with an electrooculogram recording. Similarly, a ghost may gain perception of time if they become self aware. (LaBerge, S. (2000). "Lucid dreaming: Evidence and methodology", Behavioral and Brain Sciences).

Awareness and Control

Dream control and dream awareness are related, but do not require each other. Studies have further shown that in some cases where the dreamer became lucid and aware they could exercise control, they choose simply to observe instead of interacting. (Kahan T., LaBerge S. (1994). "Lucid dreaming as metacognition: Implications for cognitive science").

The actual ability to become self aware in a dream is difficult. In 1992, a study by Deirdre Barrett examined whether lucid dreams contained four "corollaries" of lucidity:

1. The dreamer is aware that they are dreaming

2. Objects disappear after waking

3. Physical laws need not apply in the dream

4. The dreamer has a clear memory of the waking world

It was found that less than 25% of subjects tested exhibited all four. While the second, third and fourth factors were present, the first was absent, with more than 75% missing the realization that "I'm dreaming". Not surprisingly, ghost interactions seem to range in the same statics, missing the realization that "I have died".

False Awakening

There are some other interesting phenomena that occur with the mind in dreams. One is called false awakening. In a false awakening, one dreams that they have awoken. Often times the room they falsely wake up in is the same, or similar to the room they fell asleep in. This is because it is the last location the mind recalls before entering the dream state. It may also be why ghosts tend to remain and manifest in the same locations they remember, causing specific places to become "haunted" with their presence. In the living, if the person is lucid in their dream, they often believe that they are no longer dreaming and begin their morning routine. They remain unaware of the dream until they realize they haven't actually woken up, or they wake up again. Likewise, ghosts go on with what seems to them their usual behavior, remaining unaware they are dead.

Sleep Paralysis/Night Hags

Sleep paralysis is another phenomenon, but only applies to the living, as it is a side effect of the physical body. Normally during sleep the brain paralyzes the body (with the exception of heart and breathing) as a protection mechanism to prevent movements that occur in a dream from causing the physical body to move. This mechanism is usually triggered before or during sleep. However, it can sometimes continue for a short period after normal sleep while the brain awakens. When it happens this way, it causes a state where the awakened sleeper feels paralyzed. This has been mistaken by many people for being attacked by something called a "Night Hag". Sometimes it is accompanied by hallucinations, especially auditory ones that make it seem more real. These are called hypnagogic hallucinations. The effects of sleep paralysis include a feeling of heaviness or inability to move the muscles, rushing or pulsating noises, and momentary hypnogogic or hypnopompic images. I personally experienced this once years ago. It was a disturbing event because at the time I did not have knowledge of sleep paralysis phenomena. It was in the morning after a normal night's sleep. I recall waking up in my bed, but felling paralyzed, and hearing the sound of rushing air. I also had a hallucinatory feeling that I was sinking into my bed, and tried to call out, but was unable to. The entire occurrence only lasted a few seconds, but while it was happening it all seemed very real. Without knowing about what this actually is, it can be quite disturbing. It is understandable that a person could mistake this for some type of unpleasant interaction with a malevolent supernatural entity.

Out-of-Body Experience

An out-of-body experience (OBE) usually involves a sensation of being or floating outside of one's body. It may also be referred to as astral projection. In some cases people have reported seeing their own physical body from a place outside of themselves. This is called autoscopy. Out-of-body experiences are not uncommon. Approximately one in ten people claim to have had an out-of-body experience at some time in their lives. ("First Out-of-body Experience Induced In Laboratory Setting", sciencedaily.com). There is on-going research of this occurrence. Some findings by neurologists studying the phenomenon suggest that these experiences are caused by the same brain mechanisms that control lucid dreams. (Wolchover, Natalie (2012). "Near-Death Experiences are Lucid Dreams, Experiment Finds", livescience.com). Although there are some similarities in their occurrence and they way they are induced, EEG studies do not show an equivalence between out-of-body experiences and lucid dreaming. Lucidity is directly associated with stage 1 REM sleep, while out-of-body experiences are far less consistent. On EEG scans they tend to inconsistently resemble either stage 3 sleep, a waking, eyes-closed state or some other uncategorized states. While this may suggest that OBEs are a type of lucid dream taking place in a dream environment that looks like the actual environment of the dreaming subject, it does not support the idea that some conscious form of the dreamer actually leaves the body and perceives their external environment while still in a sleeping state. This is currently a debatable topic in neuroscience.

9 WHAT HAPPENS WHEN YOU DIE

When exactly is a person dead? The electrical status of the brain determines this. Death occurs when all brain activity ceases. This is known in the medical field as "brain death". We can measure when brain death occurs using a device called an EEG. EEG stands for electroencephalograph, which measures the electrical activity in the brain. The brain itself is composed of nerve cells called neurons, and support cells that provide a frame work for the neurons. When the neurons are active and firing during life, there is a nonstop pattern of electrochemical impulses. The electrical patterns are detected and recorded by the EEG.

In some cases, to confirm brain death physicians may order an EEG along with some other studies, such as cerebral blood flow or atropine test. The cerebral blood flow test involves IV injection of a radioactive drug followed by a nuclear scanning image of the brain. If no radioactivity is seen, it indicates there is no blood flow to the brain. The atropine test is also an IV injection, but is not radioactive. In a living person, atropine acts on the brain to speed up the heart, but in a brain dead patient, there is no change in heart rate, despite the administration of atropine. The EEG is the most direct method of measurement. It is very sensitive and can directly detect the smallest amounts of electrical activity in the brain, called microvolts. Even a patient in a coma will have some electrical activity that is detected by an EEG.

When you die, all electrical activity in the brain ceases. This is when a diagnosis of "brain death" is made. This is not something that happens over a long period of time. It occurs at a particular instant. A patient cannot be "almost" brain dead. You are either alive, or dead. Of course a patient's body can be kept technically alive on life support, but without electrical activity in the brain, they are essentially dead, and once the life support is removed the other body functions stop as well.

A research study published in the *Journal of Palliative Medicine*, by Dr. L.S. Chawla, et al.,

(2009), used Bispectral Index monitoring on a series of terminally ill patients who consented to the study. The patients' brainwaves were monitored before and during their times of death. In each patient, after a drop in systemic blood pressure, there was a decline in the bispectral index activity of the brain with an unexplainable transient spike. This was then followed by termination of electrical activity in the brain. This spike could be an energy signal picked up by the conversion of physical particles to pure mass less energy leaving the brain upon death. In one patient, following the spike was a period of burst suppression, before flat lining of the EEG occurred. Burst suppression is a series of spiking high activity waves followed by a period of suppressed activity, in a rhythmic pattern. It is similar to what is seen in a coma patient. It's possible that the conscious singularity in this patient did not wish to leave the physical body behind, and so lingered for a moment before moving on.

Everyone dies from "brain death". There are many possible causes, whether accidental or natural, but the end result that causes actual death is the termination of all electrical activity in the brain. This moment of death can be seen if an EEG device is attached to the patient. There is a definitive moment when all electrical activity ceases and all channels become flat lined.

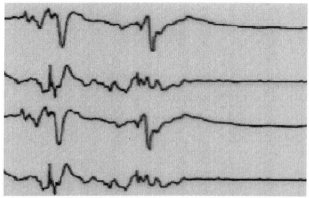

Figure 9.1 EEG showing electrocerebral silence occurring at the time of death

It is at this moment that the Higgs boson is invoked and mass is lost from the brain as the quantum conscious held in the microtubules of the brain is converted to pure, mass less energy and leaves the body. The conscious, being recently discovered existing as orchestrated objective reduction, is believed to be able to leave the physical structure of the brain. Once outside the body, it is what I refer to as a conscious singularity, or what some would call a ghost. Whether it moves on to another plane of existence is still not completely understood, and there are several theories regarding that, but it could also remain present in this plane and manifest later to be seen again. Although it is difficult to detect this energy outside of the body, we do know it exists in the physical brain during life due to the newly discovered mechanism of OOR.

10 OOR

A recent breakthrough in the field of Quantum Mechanics has found that the human conscious exists in a form of both matter and energy in the neurons of the brain, and that it is possible for it to leave the brain in the form of quantum energy. The findings combines approaches from diverse angles of molecular biology, neuroscience, quantum physics, pharmacology, philosophy, quantum information theory and quantum gravity.

Dr. Stuart R. Hameroff is the Director of the Center for Consciousness Studies, and Professor Emeritus for the Department of Anesthesiology, College of Medicine, University of Arizona and Department of Psychology Banner – University Medical Center Tucson. He, along with his colleague, theoretical physicist Sir Roger Penrose, have theorized that consciousness comes from quantum activity inside human brain cells, called OOR (Orchestrated Objective Reduction). Recently, the discovery of warm temperature quantum vibrations in microtubules within brain neurons by the research group led by Anirban Bandyopadhyay, PhD, at the National Institute of Material Sciences in Tsukuba, Japan and now at MIT, confirms their theory. In addition, it suggests that EEG rhythms, the origins of which have long been a mystery, are also derive from deeper level microtubule quantum vibrations. Furthermore, research from the laboratory of Roderick G. Eckenhoff, MD, at the University of Pennsylvania, suggests that anesthesia, which selectively erases consciousness while sparing non-conscious brain activities, has its effect via the microtubules as well in brain neurons.

The microtubules themselves are major structural skeletal components of all cells, and are found spanning the internal environment of each body cell in several different directions. However, in the neurons of the brain, their arrangement is different, where they exhibit highly organized patterns with polarized ends. This is only seen in the nerve cells of the brain, not in the rest of the body. Orchestrated objective reduction quantum bits can be seen as helical pathways in these microtubule lattices.

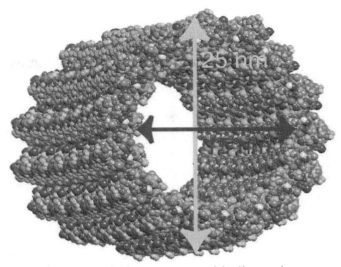

Figure 10.1 Microtubule structure with dimensions in nanometers

Because this particular configuration is only found in the cells of the brain, and not in the other cells of the body, the brain is what then houses the conscious. Some may even refer to it as being the place where the 'soul' resides. It is well protected as the brain is the only organ entirely encased in solid bone on all sides. If a person loses a part of their body, an arm or leg for example, no part of the 'soul' would be lost because it resides in the brain, protected within the skull. What about phantom limb pain?

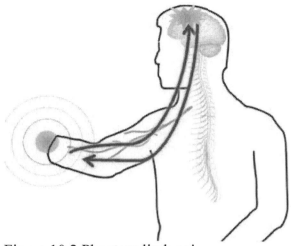

Figure 10.2 Phantom limb pain

Some believe that even though the physical part of the arm or leg is gone, the 'soul' portion is still present and can be felt. This is actually caused by damaged nerve endings at the site of amputation. They send pain signals back to the brain, which misinterprets them as coming from the nerves in the missing limb. Pain signal misinterpretation is not uncommon and can occur as referred pain as well. An example would be having pain in the left arm during a heart attack. There is nothing wrong with the left arm, but the nerves traveling up the arm and neck to the brain happen to merge with nerves coming up from the heart. When the brain receives the pain signal from the heart, it misinterprets part of the signal as coming from the left arm, and so it is felt there as well. Fortunately, the quantum energy that forms the conscious through objective reduction resides only in the brain itself.

"Objective reduction" is also known as wave function collapse in physics. It is what happens in quantum mechanics when a wave function reduces to a single observable state from superposition, (a form where a particle occupies both states at once). Physicist Roger Penrose explains it by reconciling general relativity and quantum theory. He suggests that curved space-time is not continuous, but discrete, and that each quantum superposition particle has its own space-time curvature, like a bubble in space-time. He suggests that gravity has a destabilizing effect on these bubbles causing them to collapse to one particle state. Penrose has proved this indeterminacy principle mathematically by the following equation:

$$\tau \approx \hbar / E_G$$

Where τ is the time until OR occurs, $\hbar$ is a reduced Planck constant (a physical constant that is the central quantum action in quantum mechanics), and E_G is the gravitational self-energy or the degree of space-time separation given by the superpositioned mass.

Quantities associated with measurements, such as

particle momentum, can be derived from wave function. It is a vital entity in quantum physics and is important in all modern theories, like quantum field theory incorporating quantum mechanics. The most common symbols for a wave function in equations are the Greek letters ψ and Ψ. They are what we see as quantum energy patterns in the helical pathways of the microtubules in the brain.

OOR is what we now believe to be the root of human conscious. It is also what many may call the human soul. Therefore, it may stand to reason that upon the moment of death, it is those specific parts of the microtubules that lose their mass to the Higgs field and transition from matter to a pure energy state, leaving the body, resulting in the 21 gram loss, as previously mentioned. It may be called a spirit, ghost or even a soul, but objectively I refer to it as a conscious singularity.

Reinforcing this is the fact of molecular weight regarding the microtubules themselves. Microtubules are composed of smaller subunits called tubulin. There are two kinds of tubulin, alpha (α) and beta (β). They are molecules with a complicated structure that are composed of protein strands and coiled helical sheets of amino acids (Figure 10.3).

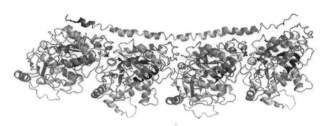

Figure 10.3 Beta tubulin molecular structure

These are represented fundamentally as single spherical units in the previous figure showing the microtubule structures. The individual atoms that make each molecule in the tubule has a weight. These molecular weights are measured in units called Atomic Mass Units, or Daltons. One subunit of tubulin by itself weighs between 55 and 60 kDa (kilodaltons), that is 55,000 to 60,000 Daltons each. As we go through life making and storing memories, the microtubules are imprinted with that information stored in specific locations on the microtubules in the form of phosphorylations. In addition, there are also other structures attached at these specific sites that help form memories, called Tau proteins. With the accumulation of these, the atomic weight of the tubulin increases to about 63 kDa each.

Alpha and beta tubulin bind together to form pairs that are called tubulin dimers. These dimers then have a combined weight of about 126 kDa (126,000 Daltons). In each neuron in the brain, there are approximately one billion tubulin dimers forming the microtubule structures. If you multiply that by the approximate number of neurons in the human brain, which is one hundred billion, you get a combined total weight of 126×10^{23} (126 hundred billion billon) Daltons. This is the weight of the microtubules that house the consciousness. It just so happens that if you convert Daltons to grams, this number of Daltons is equal to <u>21 Grams</u>. The same mass that had been scientifically attributed to the human soul by Dr. Duncan MacDougall.

11 21 GRAMS

An experiment performed by a Dr. Duncan
MacDougall in the early 1900's attempted to detect
evidence of anything unusual leaving the body upon
dying. He was a well respected physician in
Haverhill, Massachusetts who sought to measure the
mass lost by a human when the soul departed the
body at the time of death, using a specially
constructed scale. In 1901, Dr. MacDougall
measured the mass change of six patients at the
moment of death. They were all terminally ill
patients, and consented to participating in the
research. His first subject lost three-fourths of an
ounce, which is the equivalent of 21 grams.

*"Suddenly, coincident with death, the beam end
dropped with an audible stroke hitting against the*

lower limiting bar and remaining there with no rebound. The loss was ascertained to be three-fourths of an ounce."

The second patient had the same results. In subsequent tests, four of his six other patients also lost a similar amount of weight at the moment of death.

" The instant life ceased the opposite scale pan fell with a suddenness that was astonishing – as if something had been suddenly lifted from the body. Immediately all the usual deductions were made for physical loss of weight, and it was discovered that there was still a full ounce of weight unaccounted for."

He weighed these patients while they were in the process of dying from tuberculosis. He chose these patients for two reasons. First, at the time there was no known cure for tuberculosis, so these patients died naturally. Second, at the time of death in a tuberculosis patient, there is no abrupt muscle or body movements, so the scale would not be disturbed and thus give a much more accurate reading. Also, in patients with this disease, it was relatively simple to determine when death was only a few hours away. At this point the entire bed was placed on a specially made Fairbanks scale which was sensitive to two-tenths of an ounce. In the presence of four other physicians, he carefully weighed the patients before and after death. All five physicians took their own measurements and compared their results. As predicted, the same lost occurred with the other patients. He took his results to support his hypothesis that the 'soul' had mass, and when the 'soul' departed the body, so did this mass somehow. His results were published in the Journal of the American Society for Psychical Research and the medical journal American Medicine.

Of course this was carried out near the turn of the century, at a time when no one even knew of the existence of the Higgs boson or its ability to transfer mass. However, we now know that the mechanism of transferring mass from an unseen field to a massless energy particle is in fact possible, and can now be applied to Dr. MacDougall's findings.

Looking further at his results, there was an interesting variation in the third patient.

"I believe that in this case, that of a phlegmatic man slow of thought and action, that the soul remained suspended in the body after death, during the minute that elapsed before its freedom. There is no other way of accounting for it, and it is what might be

expected to happen in a man of the subject's temperament."

In this patient, there was no loss of weight immediately at death; but after one minute the patient did lose about one ounce, as if the soul did not want to leave and remained suspended in the body, but then decided or realized that it must leave. Upon leaving, mass was transferred out of the body and recorded as a loss of about one ounce. There were some who questioned the findings, but all five physicians did account for loss of air from the lungs, which was negligible; and body fluids and bowel contents which would still have remained on the patient or the bed and not have resulted in a sudden change in the scales measurements.

The opponents to his theory attempted to claim that the loss was due to perspiration because of the body temperature rising at the time of death, without lung ventilation to cool the body. This explanation was, of course, completely wrong. Obviously much more is known now about medicine and physiology than was at that time. Upon death, the body temperature begins to fall immediately, not rise. Nor do the lungs provide any mechanism of cool. Also, dead bodies do not sweat. Even if they did, perspiration occurs slowly, and would not account for an entire 21 grams of weight to be suddenly lost, because sweat remains on the surface of the skin, and so would not cause a drop in weight. Eventually sweat does evaporate, but over a period of time, and would not produce an instantaneous change. Loss of other body fluids or fecal matter would also not account for the loss as that material would still remain on the bed and would not change the weight of the scale at all.

Another argument was that air left the lungs at the moment of death. The volume of air leaving the lungs is irrelevant as tidal and reserve volumes of air were passing in and out of the lungs while the patient was still alive and breathing, which did not cause the beam on the scale to move at all. In addition, when a person stops breathing, the tidal volume that leaves the lungs is only about five hundred ml, which weighs less than half a gram. The loss documented was 21 grams, so this would not account for what occurred.

Following the results of the experiment and consulting with the other attending physicians, it was concluded that the soul weighed 21 grams. With the discovery of the Higgs boson, and OOR in the microtubules of the brain there is now evidence to support this theory. While energy can gain mass and become matter; matter can also lose mass and become massless energy. This conversion at the time of death explains the experiment's findings. The matter, of course being part of the microstructure of the brain containing the recently discovered quantum vibrations in Dr. Hameroff's findings, giving us a newly discovered scientific aspect of human consciousness.

12 THE CONSCIOUS

The complexity of the conscious is amazing. For years psychologists and philosophers have argued over whether the conscious mind is actually a separate entity from the physical brain? It is known as The Mind Body Debate, and there are two theories: Dualism and Monism. The Dualism theory says yes it is separate; while the Monism theory says no, it is not. If it is, then it would be possible to separate them from each other. However, there was never any scientific evidence to support the idea of your conscious mind as something totally separate from your physical brain. So which theory is correct?

The answer is they are both partially correct. Until the recent discovery of orchestrated objective reduction, there was no clear evidence of a separate, quantum mind from the physical body. However, recent research has now proven the existence of patterned quantum vibrations held in the microtubule structures of CNS. It has been further theorized on these recent discoveries that these quantum energy vibrations are able to leave the physical microtubule structures of the brain cells; essentially as an organized energy that can leave the body. When it occurs at the time of death, it results in a conversion of part of the brain's mass into pure energy, a conscious singularity that leaves the body. So, during the time that we are alive, it is monism to a certain extent, as the energy is there, but physically bound to the cell structures in the living. The quantum energy that is our mind is bound in helical patterns within the microtubules of the neurons themselves. But at the time of death, those patterns in the microtubules can be converted to pure energy and liberated from the brain cells. This supports the dualism theory. While the conscious mind exists as an energy pattern of quantum vibrations in the cell structures; the physical brain acts as a kind of organized scaffold for it to reside on during life. This scaffold allows for the thoughts and emotions of consciousness to be organized and controlled. Without the scaffold of the physical brain after death, the consciousness still exists, but with less control and organization, leaving that conscious singularity, or ghost, in a kind of dream state, which, as previously stated, explains their limited interactions with the living, physical world. It is interesting to note that the word we use in medical terms to refer to the conscious is

"psyche". This actually originates from the ancient Greek word psukhe, which literally means "soul".

Along with the conscious, there are the other components which include the person's memories, the pre/subconscious as well as unconscious and emotions. The conscious is actually quite complex, and is made up of several other levels, and components. One aspect of the conscious is a phenomenon referred to as the mere-exposure effect. It states that people tend to develop a preference for things merely because they are familiar with them. This effect is sometimes referred to as the familiarity principle in psychology. This is why certain places become haunted, as the conscious of someone who has crossed over prefers to remain in a location that was familiar to them in life.

Another component of the consciousness is priming. This is an effect of implicit memory where previous experiences of a person influence later actions when they are exposed to a stimulus, either in a positive or negative way. In daily life, people rely on implicit memory every day in the form of procedural memory. This is the type of memory that allows people to automatically remember how to tie their shoes, or ride a bicycle without consciously thinking about it. It is an example of unconscious unintentional memory. Explicit memory differs as it is the part of the conscious that can intentionally recall previous experiences and information. This type of memory is more difficult to preserve and access when in the mind is in unconscious levels, such as during dreams, or even after the consciousness has left the body upon death.

Blind-sight is another fascinating ability of the mind. It refers to the ability to "see" something that isn't visible, a kind of sixth sense. Research has shown it is the ability of people who are cortically blind, due to lesions in the striate cortex of the brain, to respond to visual stimuli that they do not consciously see. The majority of studies on blind-sight are conducted on patients who have the "blindness" on only one side of their visual field. Patients are asked to detect visual stimuli that are presented to their blind side only, they don't consciously see it. Research shows that blind patients achieve a higher accuracy than would be expected from chance alone. This is termed Type 1 blind-sight, and demonstrates the ability to guess, at levels significantly above chance, aspects of a visual stimulus, such as location or type of movement, without any conscious awareness of it. It is intriguing because it shows that our behavior can be guided by sensory information of which we have no conscious awareness.

The mind itself can actually be broken down into five different levels of consciousness. The first level is conscious, where the mind is aware of itself and its surrounding environment. Next is the non-conscious level. This is what controls the automatic activities of the body in life, including adrenergic responses that lead to the "fight or flight" phenomenon. It is closely associated with strong emotional responses. The next is the preconscious. This is the part of the mind that holds information about yourself and your environment that you're not thinking about, but could be. In other words, information that is accessible to the conscious mind, but not currently being focused on. There is a fine line between this level and the next of the subconscious. This level contains information of which we are not consciously aware, but impacts our reactions and behavior. The influences of priming and mere-exposure have their effect on this level as well, and subsequently on self-projection on an entity. The fifth level is unconscious, which usually contains memories and/or emotions that are unacceptable or unpleasant to the mind, and so become repressed into it.

The conscious singularity of a deceased person carriers all of this and more, as it progresses timelessly through its existence. Understanding the basics of the mind may help investigators to manipulate it in a way as to invoke a response. If not at a conscious level, then perhaps at an emotional one, where something may manifest through a Higgs boson interaction. Triggers used by investigators have shown some success in this. They are usually an object that was likely familiar in life which could invoke an emotional response, such as a doll, or an animal. Of course, live animals are seldom considered for use in paranormal investigations, and it is often a replica, some type of realistic stuffed animal. These are reported to be effective because animals are known to everyone, and are not time period specific. However, there is no guarantee that an event will occur, but something that could invoke an emotional response might trigger a Higgs interaction. Through the Higgs, mass is conveyed and we have the opportunity to witness some type of manifestation event.

13 HIGGS BOSON

The solid matter that we are made of, and that composes everything in our world is made up of atoms, which are in turn made up of subatomic particles: Protons, Neutrons and Electrons. In addition to these, and according to the Standard Model of particle physics, there are multiple yet smaller elementary particles: Quarks, Leptons, gauge bosons and the Higgs boson. Of the Quarks and Leptons, there are actually six different types and they can occur in different combinations and numbers to form other subatomic particles, such as Mesons (which have very little interaction with our known matter) and Baryons as well as Hyperons.

Recall that the first sentence in this book was 'What is a ghost?' The answer is given as a new theory regarding the conversion of part of the brain's structure and consciousness to pure, mass-less energy through Higgs interaction. If we take a closer look at this, we may ask what these mass-less energy particles are actually composed of. The most likely answer is antiquarks. These are the antiparticles of quarks. Normally, quarks have the inherent properties of electric charge, color charge, mass and spin. Antiquarks have the same properties, but with negative values, including mass.

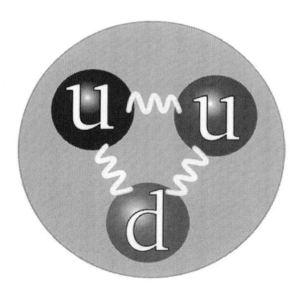

Figure 13.1 Proton structure made of three Quarks

It is interesting to note that quarks themselves are not normally observable individually because of a phenomenon in quantum physics called color confinement (involving the color charge property and the gluons holding them together). However, under certain conditions, quarks can be converted into different phases of matter and energy in a phenomenon known as quark color superconductivity. Quarks are difficult to study because such conditions to create free quarks are usually extreme and complicated to reproduce. Hopefully there will be a technology in the future that will allow us to finally detect mass less quarks. The standard model of physics includes all of the different types of quarks, as well as the leptons and bosons, Figure 13.2. These elementary particles along with the force carrier bosons are what compose all known matter.

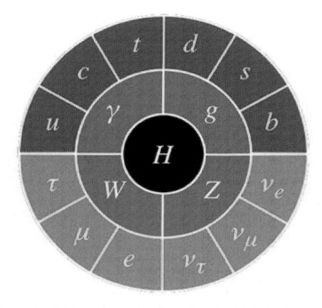

Figure 13.2 Quantum physics Standard Model

The Higgs boson is like the linchpin that holds them all together, and until recently, was only a theory. It took the Large Hadron Collider at CERN, the biggest machine ever built by man fourteen miles long and five stories tall, to detect it.

Figure 13.3 ATLAS experiment at CERN

Particle physics is a branch of physics involving the study of these constituents of matter, their structures, relationships and interactions with the environment, and each other. It also studies the elemental forces and their fields that have an effect on these particles. There are four known elemental forces in the standard model of physics: electromagnetism, strong interactive and weak interactive atomic forces and gravity. (A theory for a yet undiscovered fifth force relating to dark energy has also been postulated). These forces affect all normal matter in our universe. These forces have carrier particles called gauge bosons. The Photon is the force carrier for electromagnetism, W and Z bosons and gluons govern the strong and weak interactive atomic forces; while gravitons convey gravity.

The recently discovered Higgs Boson is probably the most significant in regard to answering our questions. It is different from all of the other particles and force carriers. All of the other particles and bosons are defined by a specific characteristic called spin. All of the matter (fermion) particles are spin-1/2, while the boson force carriers are spin-1. The Higgs boson is much different from all of the others because it is spin 0, it is referred to as a scalar. It is neither matter nor force, but something else in between. It is also thought that it may not be the only scalar particle, but one of many others yet to be discovered.

For many years it had been predicted but never seen, and was not discovered until just recently at the European Organization for Nuclear Research, better known as CERN. Because many physicists theorized about its existence but no one had been able to actually catch or create one, it was nicknamed "The God Particle" by Fermilab director Leon Lederman. Officially, it is named after Peter Higgs, a British theoretical physicist, emeritus professor at the University of Edinburgh and a Nobel Prize laureate. His research, along with another physicist, Francois Englert, concerned the theoretical discovery of a mechanism that would explain the origin of mass of subatomic particles. It turns out that there is also something else associated with the Higgs boson called the Higgs field. It is an energy field that exists everywhere in the universe. Excitation of the field will manifest as a Higgs boson, which the field uses to constantly interact with other particles. As particles pass through the field they are "given" mass. Mass itself is not generated by the Higgs field, that idea would imply creation of matter or energy which would conflict with the laws of conservation defined by Albert Einstein's famous equation ($E=mc^2$). Mass is not created but "conveyed" to particles from the Higgs field, which contains the relative mass in the form of energy. Once the field has conveyed mass to a formerly massless particle, the particle slows down because it has become heavier. This is a very important point. One may consider a massless particle to be more along the lines of a pure energy, rather than matter. But as the discoveries at CERN have proven, Higgs bosons can impart mass to a formerly massless particle. In theory, this could, in part, explain how an unseen ghost (made of some type of massless energy) could possibly invoke Higgs boson particles and obtain partial mass from the Higgs field, thereby becoming temporarily visible to the human eye.

Mathematically, it is expressed in the Lagrangian standard model equation as follows:

$$L = -\tfrac{1}{4} F_{uv} \; F \quad + i \, \Psi \, D\psi + h.c. + \psi_i \, y_i{}^j$$
$$\psi^j \phi + h.c. + |D_u \phi|^2 - V(\phi)$$

The first part of the equation represents the three forces of nature (minus gravity):

$$-\tfrac{1}{4} F_{uv} \; F$$

The next part represents the particles of matter on which these forces act:

$$i \, \Psi \, D \, \psi$$

Together, these have what is referred to mathematically in physics as symmetry. The problem is that we want to add mass to the equation, which would be written as:

$$- m \, \psi \, \psi$$

However, adding this by itself destroys the symmetry. The equation then becomes inconsistent and doesn't work. So, mathematically, to add mass to the particles without destroying symmetry, Higgs adds this:

$$+ \phi \, \psi \, \psi$$

Rewriting this expression as follows and multiplying it through, we get a mass term that works:

$$\phi = m + H$$

$$= \phi \, \psi \, \psi = (m + H) \, \psi \, \psi$$

$$= (m + H) \, \psi \, \psi = m \, \psi \, \psi + H \, \psi \, \psi$$

Where m is the constant value of the Higgs field which permeates all of space and gives rise to the mass of particles, through Higgs boson interactions.

This also explain something else, the 21 Grams Theory: the slight loss in body weight at the time of a person's death. Because the Higgs imparts mass to a formerly massless particle of energy converting it into matter, and therefore making it heavier; it also works in reverse to convert matter back to pure energy, transferring mass back to the Higgs field and therefore making it lighter, causing the recorded small loss of weight at the time of death.

14 A NEW FRONTIER FOR SCIENCE

At present, ghosts are held only in theory and considered by some to be seemingly impossible, but as we have seen in science, theory leads to great discovery. Since the discovery of the Higgs, evidence for several new theoretical and seemingly impossible particles is now being sought by various experiments at CERN. Chameleons, which are a new theoretical scalar particle, interact with matter and also have a variable effect on mass. The can also couple to photons, allowing photons and chameleons to oscillate between each other in the presence of an external magnetic field. They can be confined in hollow containers because their mass actually increases after they pass through the container wall, causing them to reflect. One approach to search experimentally for chameleons is to direct photons into a cavity, confining the chameleons produced, and then to switch off the light source. Chameleons would be indicated by the presence of an afterglow as they decay back into photons.

Magnetic monopoles and dyons, particles that have only one magnetic pole, are being researched, even though their very existence doesn't seem possible. Pions and axions, if recorded, will give science new foundations on which to base research of dark matter and dark energy. These things are not part of the standard model of physics but still exist, and learning more about axions will further our understanding of it. The discovery of the Higgs has opened doors to these and other theoretic particles, as well as the theories presented in this writing.

Pioneers in any field of scientific exploration need to approach new frontiers with open minds when seeking evidence to prove even the outmost theory. That is what the scientists at CERN are doing as they discover things in particle physics imagined but never before seen. As we learn more about the quantum physics of particles, we gain a continuous growing knowledge of the laws of nature. It is this type of approach that allows us to look in directions that we have not considered before, and to find the answers we are seeking.

As I said before, there needs to be more exploration of the real science behind ghosts, the real physics of it. Understanding the true nature of the universe and the forces that govern it require both theory and experimentation. My theory of the conscious singularity based on the link between the Higgs, OOR and twenty-one gram mass loss upon death requires the same. If we wish to know the truth of what a ghost is and what happens after death, we must start with this new theory and strive to discover more supporting evidence for it. Just as in physics, new theories bring new discoveries, and that is what will ultimately expand our knowledge and understanding of what is, as of yet, unknown.